This book is due for return on or before the last date shown above: it may, subject to the book not being reserved by another reader, be renewed by personal application, post, or telephone, quoting this date and details of the book.

HAMPSHIRE COUNTY COUNCIL
County Library

100% recycled paper

World War 2 Allied Vehicles

JOHN BLACKMAN

IAN ALLAN
Publishing

First published 1995

ISBN 0 7110 2330 1

© Ian Allan Ltd 1995

Published by Ian Allan Publishing

an imprint of Ian Allan Ltd, Terminal House, Station Approach, Shepperton, Surrey TW17 8AS.
Printed by Ian Allan Printing Ltd, Coombelands House, Coombelands Lane, Addlestone, Weybridge, Surrey KT15 1HY.

Front cover:
Most common of the Bedford QL 4x4 three-ton series was the QLD GS cargo truck. Prior to restoration this example had spent many years on a farm transporting hay bales, feed and the like, and its GS body had been replaced by a makeshift flat bed. Using as many original fittings as possible, but with new panelling and woodwork, the owner has rebuilt the vehicle as Bedford and the War Office intended. *All photographs by the author.*

Back cover top left:
This 'Jimmy' pictured on the beach at Arromanches is equipped with a radio shack and marked up as a headquarters vehicle attached to the 2nd Armoured Division.

Back cover bottom left:
Judging by the number seen at military vehicle events it sometimes seems that Dodge T214 series variants outnumber almost everything else with the exception of jeeps. Here is yet another of the breed, a Command Car, which was produced in three versions: WC56 (without winch), WC57 (with winch) and WC58 (Radio) which this vehicle appears to be. The 'S' suffix to its serial number indicates radio interference suppression equipment fitted.

Back cover right:
The M4 Sherman may not have been the best tank of World War 2 but it was certainly the most numerous. Sources differ as to exactly how many were produced but suffice to say it was well over 40,000. Of these a mere 188 were produced in Canada. Montreal Locomotive Works' version of the M4A1 was called the Grizzly and instantly recognisable by the 'G' emblem cast into its hull.

Title page:
Trundle down to the water's edge, engage the propeller drive and brave the surf. Several DUKWs crossed the English Channel in June 1994 to commemorate the 50th anniversary of D-Day.

This page:
Although not quite as common as in the aviation world, the equivalent of aircraft nose-art features on a number of military vehicles. Subject and style is also similar as can be seen from these examples (*Right and below*) of scantily clad ladies on half-tracks.

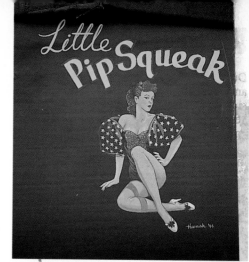

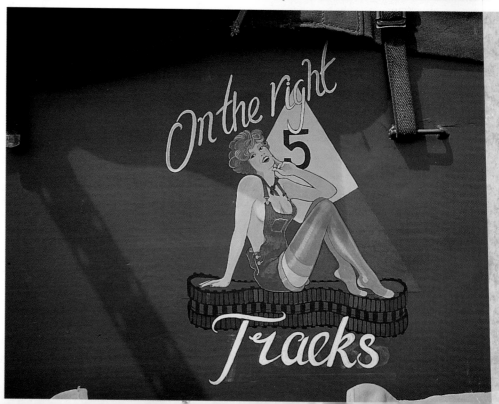

6903

Introduction

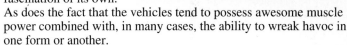

during World War 2 military vehicles were produced in numbers and of a diversity previously unimagined. As Hitler's Blitzkreig tactics showed from the outset, it was a war of mobility, largely dependant upon mechanised forces swiftly striking and counterstriking. And behind the armoured cutting edge came the myriad support and supply vehicles necessary to maintain sustained momentum.

It was also a war of high attrition. Initially, short cuts were taken to meet the numbers of vehicles required by modifying existing civilian designs. An expedient but not entirely satisfactory solution. But as time went on the Allies' industrial might proved equal to the task and vast numbers of purpose-built vehicles were produced.

Vehicle manufacturers in Canada and America, where factories operated unhindered by enemy action, were particularly well placed to meet high volume demand. In Canada, which was a Dominion member of the British Empire and therefore involved in the war from day one, arose the unusual situation of the country's three major manufacturers, all of American parentage, producing vehicles to British War Office specification. In March 1941, after having previously sold vehicles on a cash-and-carry basis, the United States Government passed the Lend-Lease Act which resulted in billions of dollars worth of military hardware and services being supplied on loan, lease, or as a gift. When the United States itself became directly involved in the war as of December 1941 an all-out effort by vehicle manufacturers big and small was necessary to produce the numbers of MVs required to satisfy the needs of both US and Allied forces.

At the war's end, with servicemen and women returning to their home countries, many of the vehicles with which history had been made were left behind, surplus to requirements. Some of these vehicles were scrapped, some were demobbed into civilian life, but first many were passed on under Military Aid Programmes to European forces whose own MV strength and production capability had been decimated. Whatever the case a sizeable number of MVs avoided the scrapman's torch, although in doing so they may have been civilianised or adapted to other tasks in a way which compromised their military pedigree.

Aesthetically speaking MVs are not the most attractive of vehicles — all olive drab and brute force — and to the uninitiated their appeal may not be immediately apparent.

But beauty is ever in the eye of the beholder and utilitarian functionalism — design entirely in the interest of function without the barest nod in the direction of appearance — holds a fascination of its own. As does the fact that the vehicles tend to possess awesome muscle power combined with, in many cases, the ability to wreak havoc in one form or another.

Perhaps aided by a general increase in the value of vintage transport, the past twenty years or so has seen the MV restoration and preservation scene steadily gain strength. Still, of the millions of vehicles built to serve during World War 2, only a tiny percentage remain. However, numbers are increasing as a growing band of enthusiasts rescue rusting and rotten hulks for painstaking restoration to a condition as good as new.

It may no longer be possible to find a World War 2 vintage truck in every French farmer's barn, but vehicles of all types are still being discovered in one condition or another. Stories of rare truck bodies being found serving as chicken sheds are not unusual and rummaging through scrapyards can still turn up some interesting artifacts. Despite the fact that such finds are likely to be in extremely poor condition, the fact is that mass production and stockpiling of spares, both new and used, means that in many cases it is still possible to get hold of the same parts that would have been fitted to a vehicle in its theatre of action 50 years ago.

Even tanks, self-propelled guns and armoured cars — once the sole preserve of museums — are now to be found in the hands of a few private individuals and companies. Seen by many as the pinnacle of the 'Green Machine' preservation movement, the number of these privately-owned heavyweights is bound to grow, albeit slowly. Judging by the advertisements in enthusiast's magazines, ready to roll armour is there for the buying — if you can afford it.

Likewise, for those who can afford it, commercial companies exist which will restore wrecks to *concours* condition to order. But most owners work on their own vehicles, frequently pooling resources and expertise with each other via clubs and societies like the Invicta Military Vehicle Preservation Society and Military Vehicle Trust. The finished articles are then proudly displayed, often in support of charitable activities, especially those for the benefit of ex-servicemen's organisations.

Particularly popular with vehicle owners, public and old soldiers alike, have been the many commemorative rallies to such fitting and evocative locations as the Normandy Beaches and Arnhem. Whatever the event, these charismatic vehicles — the ugly ducklings of the transport world unblessed by glittering chrome and aesthetic beauty — are sure of a warm welcome.

This book is not intended to be a catalogue or history of World War 2 military vehicles, since several such publications already exist. Rather, it is a photo album marking what a growing number of enthusiasts are doing to ensure the survival, in working order, of the vehicles which played leading roles in the modern world's most devastating war. From tired iron and torn canvas to living history.

Acknowledgments: Thanks are due to all the vehicle owners and drivers who, knowingly or unknowingly, assisted with the compilation of this book. Individual mention should go to members of the North Thames Branch of the Invicta Military Vehicle Preservation Society, Rod and Rex Cadman, and Marguerite Walden of the Military Vehicle Trust. Lastly a special word of thanks for the 'Bedford Boys' — Bill Dedman, Will Carpenter and Mel Coils.

Previous page:
The Sexton was designed and built in Canada and carried a British 25-pdr field gun in its open-topped welded-plate superstructure. Over 2,000 were built between 1943 and 1945 and the vehicle proved extremely popular. It served with the British army until the 1950s and was also used by South Africa, India and Portugal.

Right:
Restoration styles vary from the plain Jane to the fully loaded. This 'Jimmy' very definitely falls into the latter category. Camouflage netting, roll of barbed wire, machine gun mount and all the other paraphernalia make this vehicle stand out from the common herd.

Opposite:
Norton built over 100,000 motorbikes during World War 2. The most numerous were the 490cc single-cylinder 12bhp 16H models, of which an example is illustrated here. They were used by both the Army and Royal Air Force and sidecar equipped versions were also produced.

Opposite:
A nicely restored pair of BSA (British Small Arms) M20 motorcycles. Like the Norton 16H, the M20 employed a 12bhp air-cooled engine, but of 496cc capacity, to drive the rear wheel via a four-speed foot-change gearbox and chain.

Below:
The wearing of uniforms is a controversial issue in the world of restored military vehicles. But to ride a Military Police Harley-Davidson dressed in anything other than an approximation of a Snowdrop's uniform would be taking discretion too far. US Military Police were originally known as 'Snowdrops' because of their white helmets, but these two would-be MPs are wearing the toned down combat version.

Right:
This well-worn Harley-Davidson WLC, the version of the WLA produced for Canadian forces' use, has obviously been well-ridden by its Dutch owner since being demobbed. After the cessation of hostilities, surplus WLAs and WLCs were popular as cheap and rugged transport and are still much sort after as, arguably, the most charismatic wartime motorbike.

Above:
A variety of civilian saloon car designs were pressed into service as staff cars and VIP transports during World War 2. The most numerous in US Army service was the Ford 2GA, which was a utilitarian version of Ford's 1942 Fordor.

Opposite:
In Britain, standard civilian saloon cars were also adopted by the services with militarised versions of Humber's Super Snipe Mk2 in production between 1939 and 1944. Various body styles were available, including; saloon, tourer and; as seen here, utility.

Left:
Opinions are divided as to how the famous ¼-ton 4x4 became universally dubbed the jeep. It was probably as a result of its 'GP' (General Purpose) designation, but some suggest it was an affectionate likening to an odd Popeye cartoon character called Eugene the Jeep. Whatever the reason vast numbers — over 600,000 by US Government order alone — were produced by Ford and Willys. The many surviving examples reflect the jeep's diverse roles, but it is unlikely that a Royal Engineers vehicle ever transported 'Diamond Lil's' crew to dispersal. There is a link however; Ford manufactured both Liberators and GPWs!

Below:
Pictured in the twilight of its years but still driving well, a 1939 Morris 'Tilly' light utility which was another militarised type of saloon car. Several manufacturers produced similar vehicles which were little more than truncated civilian saloons with a utility body added. As such they make attractive restoration projects. This example has been finished in the colours of the 78th Infantry Div, 6th Battalion Royal West Kents.

Opposite:
Canada was one of the first foreign customers for the ubiquitous jeep and received in the region of 11,000 before war's end — the vast majority being Willys MBs. This better-than-new example, bearing Royal Signals Ist Infantry Division markings, exhibits some of the Canadian batch hallmarks: a single headlamp with guard (the other headlamp orifice being covered by a bridge classification plate), lifting rings on the front and rear bumpers and a tool box fitted in the space between front bumper and radiator.

Opposite:
Armed and dangerous: a Ford GPW, bristling with machine guns, is festooned with extras as befitting behind-the-lines use by the legendary SAS. This dramatic restoration faithfully replicates what was probably the vehicle's most warlike incarnation. Note the prickly beast's armoured screens for driver and gunner, long-range fuel tanks in the rear compartment and cut-down bumpers — a far cry from the majority of jeep restorations.

Left:
Over 12,000 Ford GPA amphibians were produced. These were basically boat-like hulls mated to a lengthened GPW chassis. They were heavier and had less carrying capacity than normal jeeps and were found to be of limited use in Western Europe. However, many were sent to Russia under Lend-Lease and the Soviets even built their own copy of the design. Part of the design's weakness was that it lacked freeboard and was therefore limited in its load carrying capacity. This was compounded by the fact that European rivers tend not to have conveniently sloping banks to allow the vehicle to be driven in and out of the water with any degree of ease. The GPA was therefore not as popular as might otherwise have been expected.

Left:
One step up the size and weight ladder from Humber's militarised Super Snipe variants was their 4x4 Heavy Utility, known as the 'Box'. They were made between 1940 and 1945 and, from the windscreen with rounded corners, it is possible to tell that the aptly named *Pandora* is a late production model.

Below left:
Humber based a variety of vehicles on the same 8cwt 4x4 chassis. This now unique 1939-built field ambulance is but one example. Now finished in 4th Infantry Division markings, the vehicle saw actual wartime service in Italy with an RAF Mountain Rescue unit and has taken the owner six years to restore.

Opposite:
Even more box-like than Humber's 4x4 Heavy Utility is the Chevrolet of Canada C8A Heavy Utility or HUP (Heavy Utility Personnel) for short. Almost 13,000 were produced between 1942 and 1945 and they were unusual in being the only vehicles built entirely, both chassis and body, in the General Motors-owned factory.

Above:
This 1939 Morris PU8/4 8cwt 4x4 wireless truck is a rare survivor of the 700 or so built. There was also a Personnel/GS version produced in even smaller numbers. The red wheel nuts on British Army trucks are not for decoration. They hold the two halves of the split rim wheels together and should never be undone with the tyre inflated.

Opposite:
With the exception of jeeps, US-built Dodge vehicles seem by far the most numerous subjects for preservation. However, the 1940/41 ½ ton series, such as this 1941 T207/WC4 Weapons Carrier, are far less common than the ¾ ton series that superseded them from 1942. Note the early style US roundels.

Opposite:
Pictured in the small Normandy town of Port-en-Bessin, where its desert paint looks somewhat incongruous, is a rare 1943 Canadian-built Dodge T222/D15. Behind this pristine restoration, and beneath the Vauban Tower built in 1694, is a bunker stormed by 47th (RM) Commando on the afternoon of D-Day+1.

Right:
In the foreground is a Dodge T212/D8A, a Canadian-built version of its US parent company's T207 series. The main difference was that the T212/D8A, like all Canadian produced vehicles, had right-hand drive. This rare animal was discovered in an Essex scrapyard in the early 1980s and its service history is uncertain.

Below right:
Final Dodge ½ ton 4x4 model was the T215 which was supplied in the usual comprehensive range including Weapons Carrier, Ambulance, Command Car and, as here, WC26 Carryall. They were all powered by a 230cu in six-cylinder engine capable of developing a maximum of 92bhp.

Above:
Unhindered by enemy action the Canadian automotive industry went into top gear during World War 2 and produced vast numbers of military vehicles. The companies largely concerned — Ford, General Motors and Chrysler — were all of American parentage, but the majority of MVs produced were designed in Canada to British War Office specification. These vehicles, such as the 1942 vintage Ford F15A illustrated, became known as Canadian Military Pattern (CMP) vehicles.

Opposite:
A far more warlike version of the same basic design is this Canadian-built Chevrolet C15. Fitted with aero-screen windshields and a machine gun mount, this vehicle represents one used by the Free French at Bir Hakim in Libya. The French owner admits to altering the drivetrain in the interests of economical modern motoring.

Opposite:
Between 1939 and 1945 around 66,000 Bedford MW 15-cwt 4x2s were produced. This particular 1942 example started life as a MWC Water Tanker but has been restored as an MWD GS truck — a far more common type. Although historically inaccurate for this particular example, the restoration makes the vehicle infinitely more practical when it comes to hauling camping paraphenalia and the like to vehicle rallies.

Above:
In addition to the ubiquitous GS truck, Bedford MW variants included a wireless truck, gun tractor, water bowser and MWG Anti-Aircraft Gun Portee. This 1939 example of the latter has the early series open cab and aero-screens which make for a draughty ride. Later model MWs had doors and full windscreens. Some even had totally enclosed cabs.

Right:
This beautifully finished Bedford MWG carries a pair of Mk2 Bren Guns in a Motley mount obtained from the Portuguese Army to whom they had been sold as surplus after the war. Owners must be able to produce deactivation certificates for all fire-arms, whether portable or fixed.

Opposite:
The Fordson WOT2 was, like its similar Bedford MW brethren, in production throughout World War 2 and available in all the usual variants. The 'Berlin This Way' inscription and so-called 'Mickey Mouse ears' black over khaki drab camouflage firmly dates this nice restoration as representing a post-invasion vehicle.

Following page:
The distinctive bonnet lines mark this truck as a Morris Commercial C8 GS. These 4x4 15cwt trucks were produced towards the end of the war — this particular vehicle was built in 1944 — and came with a 64bhp engine driving either the rear or all wheels via the luxury of a five-speed gearbox.

Above:
Another Dodge T214 variant was the WC53 Carryall which could take up to six passengers or light cargo. 'Only' around 8,500 of this variant were produced and they are therefore far less numerous on the restoration circuit than Weapons Carriers. The US Army routinely prefixed reconnaisance truck serials with '20', the rest of the serial indicating the vehicle's sequential number.

Top right:
During World War 2 Dodge produced a quarter of a million T214 series ³/₄ ton 4x4s. They came in a variety of variants, the most numerous of which was the WC51 Weapons Carrier. The vehicle illustrated is in fact a WC52, which is a winch equipped WC51.

Above right:
Seemingly a popular choice for the military vehicle preservationist is the WC54 Ambulance, which is yet another Dodge T214 variant. It could accommodate up to four stretcher cases or seven 'walking-wounded', and as many as 26,000 were produced between 1942 and 1945. Many were left behind in Europe by departing forces.

Opposite:
When the US Army increased the size of a rifle squad from eight to 12 men, Dodge produced stretched versions of its T214 — the 1½ ton 6x6 T223/WC62 and winch-equipped WC63. Production ran from 1942 to 1945 during which time some 44,000 were produced, most being supplied to US Forces. This interesting machine gun equipped WC63 features the 1943/45 production body of steel panelled wood.

Above:
As the name painted behind the driver's door indicates, 'Radio Flyer' is Chevrolet 1½ ton 4x4 Radio Panel truck as used by the US Army Signals Corp. This finely restored example of a rare model was shipped from the United States to the UK to take part in the 50th Anniversary of D-Day commemorations.

Left:
This unique restoration is a 1938 Fordson 817T Sussex balloon winch truck. A shining example of the sort of standards achievable and very definitely a labour of love. The owner/restorer had to track down parts from as far afield as California (where the cab was found) as well as specially fabricate unobtainable items like the rear mudguards.

Below:
Wartime Bedfords are relatively common, but this 1940 Bedford OXC artic unit is an exception. These trucks were modified by Scammell to pull semi-trailers and this particular OXC had been used for towing a fuel bowser. Released onto the civilian market in 1966, it now hauls a six-ton GS trailer.

Opposite:
This odd looking vehicle is a GMC AFKX-352 Workshop truck. Various types based on the same vehicle were produced for specific purposes including: small arms repair, instrument repair, spare parts and welding. This excellent restoration's so-called 'Mickey Mouse ears' paintwork reincarnates one of the few of this type used by the British Army.

Opposite:
GMC produced over half a million 'deuce-and-a-half' 2½ ton trucks during the war. A great many survived through being passed on by the United States to European allies and then on to the civilian market. This example is a 6x6 CCKW-352, the 145in wheelbase version.

Above:
Looking brand spanking new, this GMC CCKW-353 'Jimmy' is fresh from the paintshop and needs only a new set of canvases to be complete. Commercial restorers 'Tired Iron Truck Services' found this piece of tired iron in a French farmer's hedge, dragged it out and towed it over 300 miles back to their workshops where it was overhauled on behalf of an American client.

'Jimmies' were produced in a multitude of versions. Most of those restored are of the cargo variety but this Norwegian-owned CCKW-353 is what is known as a 'Shop Van'. In service the house-type body could have been used as a machine or repair shop and served much the same function as the AFKX-352.

Around 21,000 6x6 DUKWs (a kind of amphibious 'deuce- and-a-half') were produced between 1942 and 1945 and with the odd modification many went on to serve useful civilian roles. Some even ended up offering 'all aboard the Skylark, twice round the bay' type pleasure trips for holiday makers. Although many an overladen DUKW overturned while ferrying cargo onto the Normandy beaches 50 years ago, it is quite a stable craft. And, in June 1994, to prove the point a dozen or so crossed the English Channel under their own power.

Opposite

In 1944 hundreds, if not thousands, of GMC's famous DUKWs emerged from the sea onto Normandy beaches to bring much needed supplies to the armies fighting their way inland. Fifty years later a handful re-enacted the scene on Arromanches beach. In the background can be seen the remains of the famous Mulberry Harbour.

Above:

'Rare Breed' it says on the cab doors of this 1942-built Studebaker US6, and, compared with its 'Jimmy' cousins it is a rare breed. The 2½-ton 6x6 was produced in parallel with GMC's 'deuce-and-a-half', mainly for use by the USA's allies, the majority serving with Russian, Australian and — as represented by this preserved

example — British forces. 'Rare Breed' had been cannibalised after its military service and was purchased by its restorer in 1987 as an incomplete collection of parts. It took two years of hard work to track down everything necessary — the cab came all the way from Australia — and to return the 'Stude' to good as new condition.

Following page:

Although rated as a three-ton truck the British Bedford OY appears far less sturdy than its American cousins and shares the same engine as the 15-cwt Bedford MW. The OYs, in all their variants, were the most numerous of British-built trucks. This 1944 OYD GS is finished in the markings of the 11th Armoured Division.

Above left:
As well as the GS cargo truck there was a range of alternative QL body styles available, including the QLR Wireless truck seen here at a military vehicle rally. In the interest of commonality, if not performance, the Bedford MW, OY and QL all shared the same engine.

Left:
Austin also produced a three-ton 4x4, the K5, of which some 12,000 were produced. The 1944-built 'Skreamin' Demon' — perhaps a reference to the noisy combination of drive-train and tyres — represents a vehicle in service with the 4th Infantry Division. K5s served on all fronts during the war; amongst variations still to be seen are those fitted with canvas-topped cabs that were supplied to the 7th Armoured Division for use in the desert.

Right:
Ford's entry into the three-ton 4x4 arena was the Fordson WOT6 produced between 1942 and 1945. This 1944 machine, photographed just prior to embarking for France (hence the yellow tinted headlights), has hidden beneath its canvases two rows of bus seats making the ride tolerably comfortable, if no faster, than 50 years ago.

Opposite:
There will always be the owner who wants something just that little bit different. An example of this is the fine Austin K6A/ZH breakdown gantry illustrated here. These gantries were originally built for the British Army in 1944-45. Painted on the front right-hand mudguard, and just visible in the dawn light, is the REME arm of service badge, while on the left-hand mudguard is the camel of the 373rd Company RASC.

Left:
About a quarter of the trucks produced by Ford and Chevrolet of Canada were in the 4x4 three-ton class and of similar basic design although differing in detail, engine and drive-train. This is a 1943 Ford of Canada F60S ambulance. The odd dent in the vehicle's bodywork almost adds, rather than detracts, from the overall effect.

Opposite:
Very similar in general appearance is this Canadian Chevrolet C60S breakdown truck. It is marked with the REME (Royal Electrical and Mechanical Engineers) blue/yellow/red arm of service badge and cross-keys of the 2nd Infantry Division and is one of several fine vehicles preserved and operated by the REME Corps Museum.

Opposite:
A Ford of Canada F60S LAA-T is pictured towing a Bofors light anti-aircraft gun. Very few of the latter are in private hands. Except that they were prefixed by the letter 'C', Canadian-produced vehicles bore serial numbers commencing with a letter designating type, eg 'A' for ambulance or, in this case, 'H' for tractor.

Above:
Canadian Military Pattern 4x4 three-ton trucks are relatively common, but this three-ton 6x6 C60X is quite a rarity. Apparently 2,710 were built between 1942 and 1944, of which many were exported. The chassis was similar to that of the 4x4 C60L but fitted with a larger capacity, higher performance engine.

Above left:
'King-Kong', a Federal 94x43C ⁴/₅-ton 4x4 tractor, is a rare survivor of the 8,000 or so 94x43A, B and C models produced between 1941 and 1945. The B and C models had an open cab and this particular example of a 1943 C model is hitched to a contemporary vintage Fruehaf K78 radar van and appropriately marked as serving with the United States Army Air Force.

Above right:
Between August and December 1944 a stream of trucks shuttled between St Lô in Normandy and supply dumps feeding the advancing Allied armies. Initially the route

of the so-called 'Red Ball Express' took trucks, such as this Diamond T four-ton 6x6 Cargo, to a dump on the outskirts of Paris. But as the Allied armies split, so the 'Red Ball Express' route followed, one arm extending northeast to Soisson, the other east to Sommesous.

Opposite:
This 1944 Morris-Commercial C8 Quad MkIII field artillery tractor is privately owned, but the 25-pounder and limber belong to the Royal Armouries. The Morris Quad was in production from 1939, but it was in 1944 that the box-like body seen here was introduced to replace the earlier multifaceted beetle-back type.

Left:
Related to the
Morris-Commercial
C8, and a
particularly good —
not to say unusual —
restoration, is this
C9/B Self-Propelled
40mm Bofors anti-
aircraft gun carrier.
Note the stabilising
jacks and open four-
seater cab. Much
effort has gone into
this fine vehicle.

Opposite:
Although there were
several versions of
AEC's Matador —
including tanker,
flatbed, armoured
anti-tank gun carrier
and command
vehicle — the
majority of the
10,000 or so built
served as medium
artillery tractors.
This 1943 AEC
Matador 0853 wears
the red-over-blue
Royal Artillery arm
of service marking
combined with the
11th Armoured
Division's formation
sign.

Opposite:
'Helen', a 1944 Albion CX22S 6x4, takes us into the realm of the heavy artillery tractor — with the accent on heavy. She weighs in at almost 24,000lb and those large fuel tanks give an indication of just how thirsty is her 9,080cc diesel engine. Only about 500 of these heavyweights were produced.

Above:
The US-built Mack NM6 6x6 was 1,000lb lighter than the Albion but had the advantage of 6x6 traction and an engine capable of developing 50% more bhp. Most of the NM5 to NM8 series trucks were produced for Lend-Lease and Great Britain took some 2,300 of the beasts as heavy artillery tractors.

Opposite:
Speaking of beasts, here are a couple of Scammell Pioneer SV/2s heavy breakdown tractors which answer that description — at least according to the name 'The Beast' one proudly bears above its windscreen. At the end of their service lives these vehicles proved popular with haulage companies and anyone whose business required real automotive muscle power. Hence quite a few have survived.

Above right:
As ever, US-built breakdown trucks went one better in terms of size, weight and power. Both Ward LaFrance and Kenworth produced variations of the same basic M1 Heavy Wrecker design. This is an early model Kenworth 570 M1 that seems to have acquired a late model 'tree-wrecker' bumper somewhere in its long career.

Below right:
In 1943 heavy wrecker design was standardised with the result that the Kenworth 573 and Ward LaFrance 1000 Series 5 (of which 'Zadok' is one) became virtually identical. The heavier and more angular vehicle came with an open cab and was designated M1A1.

Above:
A heavy wrecker doing what heavy wreckers do best — rescuing a broken down Bedford QL. After the war many of these vehicles were passed on to European forces with whom, because of their specialised role and limited usage, they have served until quite recently.

Left:
It is just as well that there is always someone around intent on preserving the esoteric, not to say downright unusual, such as this Swedish-owned Brockway C666 crane truck. About 1,300 of these 6x6 six-ton trucks fitted with a Quickway four- to eight-ton crane were supplied between 1943 and 1945.

Below:
In a similar vein is this Brockway B666 bridge erector based on the same chassis as the C666. On the truck bed, where once would have been carried pontoons ready to be lifted into position by the four-ton hoist, now sits a Studebaker M29 'Weasel'. Both vehicles are a credit to their owner.

Above:
'Mighty White', a 1942 White 666 six-ton cargo truck, is hauling a La Crosse flat bed trailer on which is loaded a 1943 International M5 high speed tractor commonly used for towing artillery. Although painted in US Army livery, the most un-American phrase 'had nowt taken out' painted on the monster's flanks gives the game away as to the owner's nationality.

Opposite:
Boys don't grow up they just get bigger toys... and they don't come much bigger or more impressive than this — a 1942 Diamond T 980 12-ton 6x4 tractor and Rogers trailer hauling a Sherman M4A1 Grizzly. The tractor/trailer combined to form the M19 tank transporter and was originally produced to meet British needs.

Above:
Arguably some of the most impressive vehicles ever built were the Pacific Car & Foundry M26 armoured 12-ton tractors produced in 1943/44. Here are no less than two of the breed: one restored but in need of 'tidying' after a winter in the open, the other unrestored and still in the livery of its previous owner, a French haulage company. Linked to a semi-trailer the M26 became the M25 'Dragon Wagon' tank transporter.

Right:
A fine example of aircraft type nose art that adorned some wartime vehicles, 'King Kong' on a Federal tractor unit.

Opposite:
Between 1941 and 1945 29,000 Universal Carriers were built in Canada to augment production in the UK, Australia and New Zealand. Several different variants were produced including mortar and anti-tank gun carriers, but this is the plain and simple Ford C01UC. Steering is accomplished by displacement of the front bogie unit for gentle turns or by track braking for sharper changes of direction.

Opposite:
The smile on the driver's face says it all. The Studebaker M29 'Weasel' is a fun vehicle (albeit built with a serious intent). Although there was a truly amphibious version produced, the M29C with a boat like hull incorporating buoy cells and twin rudders, the driver of this M29 had no qualms about tackling the odd few feet of seawater as he showed off its capabilities on Arromanches beach.

Left:
White M3 scout cars are popular; they have the cachet of being armoured yet are reasonably easy to maintain. A total of 21,000 were originally built and they were widely used by Allied forces during and after World War 2. The Greek army sold off 21 of them a year or two ago so now is probably the time to pick one up at a bargain price!

Opposite:
During World War 2 the half-track concept was popular with both the Allies and the Axis forces. In the United States three companies joined together to standardise on design and production: White, Autocar and Diamond. The resulting M2, and longer wheelbase M3 as captured here, spawned a series of variants.

Above:
As ever larger numbers were required, particularly for Lend-Lease, the International Harvester Corp also started to produce half-tracks closely based on the White/Autocar/Diamond product, but with various differences. Most obvious, and apparent from the M9 (International's version of the M3) illustrated, were flat section front mudguards and rounded corners to the rear body.

Left:
After the war surplus half-tracks went on to serve for many years with the forces of, amongst others, France, the Netherlands, Belgium and Israel, so helping to ensure the survival of a representative number. One particularly successful variant of the basic M3/M9 was the quad 0.50 calibre machine gun armed White M16 and International M17 equivalent. This recently restored M16 features a fully operational turret.

Opposite:
Best known British-built armoured car of World War 2 is the Daimler Dingo. With normally only a single Bren gun for armament, the lightly armoured vehicle was capable of a sprightly performance courtesy of its five forward and five reverse gears. Postwar, many examples went on to serve with UN Forces in Korea and various Third World armies. Several are privately owned and this particular vehicle bears the famous red jerboa of the 7th Armoured Division.

Opposite:
When production of Daimler Dingos could not keep up with demand the Rootes Group was asked to design and build a similar vehicle. For ease of production many components were taken or adapted from Humber 4x4 military vehicles already in production. The resulting Humber Mk1 scout car was less sophisticated than the Dingo and had lighter armour, but was capable of a healthy 62mph.

Above left:
This Fox Mk1 armoured car is a Canadian-built machine gun armed version of the Humber MkIV armoured car. They could be fitted with guns of either 0.30 or 0.50 calibre and a total of 1,500 were produced in 1942/43 powered by rear mounted GMC 270 engines and fitted with hulls and turrets built by the Hamilton Bridge Co. Fox Mk1s were used in several theatres of war including Italy from where this vehicle's current owners hail.

Below left:
Daimler's Mk 1 and the improved Mk II (illustrated) were arguably the most successful of British World War 2 armoured cars. When under development in 1939/40 the intention was to incorporate the performance, armour and armament of a contemporary light tank into a wheeled chassis. In fact the turret and two-pounder gun were similar to those used on the Tetrach light tank. An interesting feature is the provision of a second, rearward facing driver's position.

Opposite:
Introduced in 1943, the Ford M8 light armoured car was considered by the US Army to be both undergunned and underarmoured for its intended role. Nevertheless it served through the Korean War before being phased out by the US Army and went on to equip European and Third World forces for many years. In British service M8s were known as 'Greyhounds' because of their 56mph top speed.

Right:
The M20 is more or less a turretless M8 armed with a ring mounted 0.50 calibre machine gun. It is said that spares are relatively easy to come by and the vehicles easy to maintain by virtue of their simple and rugged design so these vehicles make for popular restoration projects. The Los Angeles Police Department apparently keeps a battering-ram-equipped M20 on strength to force doors during drug raids!

Cadillac, a division of GMC, put the M5 tank into production in 1942 to supercede the M3. It was powered by a pair of V8 car engines driving the front sprockets through a pair of automatic Hydramatic transmissions and was capable of almost 40mph. Various improvements resulted in the marginally larger M5A1 Stuart pictured here.

Left:
The M5 Stuart proved undergunned and underarmoured in combat and was declared obsolete by the US Army in 1944. As is the way of these things, many M5s and M5A1s were given or sold to Allied forces postwar and quite a few have since ended up in collector's hands. Their automotive-based drive train is an advantage when it comes to ease of maintenance. 'Kraut Crusher' makes easy work of what was once a Ford Escort. Hardly surprising that as restorations go, this M5A1 Stuart is a little worn around the edges. But the crew are having fun and the crowd are roaring their approval so what's the odd scratch and dented track guard?

Above:
'Athanasia', an M4A2 maintained by the Friends of the Tank Museum, Bovington, features the 76mm gun and turret developed to replace the first generation Sherman's 75mm gun. The higher velocity weapon was an improvement, but it was still unable to cope effectively with the German Tiger or Panther tanks.

Opposite:
Grizzlys all possessed cast, as opposed to welded flat plate, hulls and were built in the latter part of 1943 before being discontinued when US production proved unable to meet demand. The uninformed watching one of these being started from cold might wonder why a crew member first energetically cranks what appears to be a large starting handle protruding from the tank's rear hull. Nothing to do with clockwork power, the Grizzly's engine is an air-cooled radial which must be turned over before firing-up to remove any oil that might have gathered in the cylinders. There are in the region of 50 Shermans in private hands and in Europe the majority appear to be Grizzlys. This is probably because a Welsh dealer purchased several dozen of them from surplus Portuguese army stocks in the early 1980s. Although their gun barrels had been lopped off, they were mostly in reasonable condition.

Above right:
From 1944 onwards Shermans were produced with a redesigned track and suspension. Tanks fitted with the new horizontal volute suspension system (HVSS) were known as 'Easy Eights'. Improved system or not, this M4 A1 'Easy Eight' ran into trouble when it returned to Arromanches to take part in the 50th Anniversary of D-Day commemorations and was alleged to have damaged several kilometres of road!

Below right:
The M7 self-propelled 105-mm howitzer (known as 'Priest' in British service because of its pulpit-style machine gun mount) was introduced in 1942. It was based on both the M3 and M4 chassis with an open topped hull and was widely used by US and Allied forces in most theatres of war.

Opposite:
Like all Canadian-built vehicles the Sexton has right-hand drive. As in the case of the Grizzly, most of the surviving Sextons last served with the Portuguese army and were sold off to dealers in the 1980s. This fully-restored example now bears the markings of the 50th Infantry Division.

Left:
Sure to make even the most trouble-prone collector forget the trials and tribulations of owning World War 2 armour is to take part in an event like the 50th Anniversary Parade through Bayeux, first major town to be liberated after D-Day. Here the crews of a trio of Grizzlys and a Sexton relax after carefully steering their vehicles through Bayeux's narrow streets.

Opposite:
A Ford GPW leading three British-built Bedfords somewhere in Britain (as they used to say) 1994. The Bedfords, an MW, OY and QL, are painted in matching 11th Armoured Division markings. Did they ever look so good 50 years ago?

Above:
The real thing. A 'Dizzy' T968 Cargo. Pure trucking muscle-power!

Opposite:
The four-wheel drive Dingo was capable of a nifty performance in both its five forward and five reverse gears — the latter were a feature popular with any crew obliged to make a speedy retreat. Over 6,500 were produced with many serving long after World War 2 until being finally replaced by the Ferret. This particular example is part of the collection of the Imperial War Museum at Duxford.

F 209485

54

Above:
The restoration of a vehicle is not complete until all the correct bits of equipment are found and stowed. Genuine period artifacts are hard to come by and attract a price premium, but modern reproductions form an adequate alternative.